Young of the Faith

John E. Barba

WestBow
PRESS
A DIVISION OF THOMAS NELSON

ISBN: 978-1-4497-4245-4 (sc)

Library of Congress Control Number: 2012909675

WestBow Press books may be ordered through booksellers or by contacting:

WestBow Press
A Division of Thomas Nelson
1663 Liberty Drive
Bloomington, IN 47403
www.westbowpress.com
1-(866) 928-1240

Printed in the United States of America

WestBow Press rev. date: 5/29/2012

Don't let anyone look down on you
because you are young, but set an example for the
believers in speech, in life, in love, in faith, and in purity.
1 Timothy 4:12

ACKNOWLEDGEMENTS

I would like to thank my pastors, Chad McCartney, Tom Schmidt, and James Mendoza, for their amazing leadership and love, which continuously pours into my life.

To my mentors: Pablo Longi, Steve Paulson, Dan Magura, Jim Walker, and Tano Tijerina.

A special thanks to my big brothers in the faith: Zeke DeLeon and Caye Tijerina.

Like a father to me: Carlos Sr. Arredondo.

Mom, I thank God that He chose you to be my mother in this life! Kim and Gina: I love you both! Baby Kaylee and Kaytlin, you're the cutest!

FOREWORD

A few years back, a young man I had watched become a believer in my church came up to me and asked me to train him. He had heard I knew a lot about Eschatology (end times theology) and wanted some one-on-one tutoring on the subject. Several years later, we had worked through the end times and the book of Acts as well, with him bringing a friend or two along the way. I was quite impressed that this kid who didn't really know me would have the audacity to come and ask for help from me. It was pretty cool—very New Testamentish. That's the way you were trained then: find someone you respect and let him know you were interested in his training, and see what happens.

As John and I trained, he became a cross between a little brother and a son and a trusted friend. I am proud to say he serves the Lord with his entire being. As he has grown up in the Lord, he has learned much, not just from me, but from a number of godly men who have both knowledge and wisdom in spiritual things and worldly affairs.

In this short book, John speaks as an older brother, giving easily read and easily digested advice on living a successful life to his younger brothers about to hit the world. It lays out many essentials of living life in a manner pleasing to God. It is also filled with tips for living the type of life that bears fruit and avoids spiritual pitfalls that plague humanity.

Whether a young person starting out, or an older person just finding out about the new life in Christ, you will find this book to be a great source of realistic encouragement of how to live life. I highly recommend learning from it and finding someone to teach it to!

Steve Paulson

INTRODUCTION

My name is John Eric Barba, and I'm twenty-four years old. I am a believer and follower of Jesus Christ. At an early age, by the grace of God, I came to know Him and have developed a personal relationship with Him. I know there are thousands and thousands of young people who have made the decision to trust and follow God; however, it doesn't end there. As a matter of fact, it is the beginning of a race set out for us: a race filled with trials and joy, with decisions and guidance, with failures and also hope, a hope that is found in our redeemer, Jesus Christ. Who said that you need to be a certain age to serve and worship our God, or that God couldn't use you at an early age to lead, to preach, to evangelize, and to set the example for the believers? Do we understand that by the power and strength of God, we have the ability to glorify His name no matter our age? The real question is, are we going to be obedient to our Father? When we enter high school, we are ready for the work, football games, boyfriends and girlfriends. Or maybe it's senior year and we are getting ready to look at what college we want to attend, but we're just going through the motions spiritually. Then we tell ourselves, "And later, I will be mature enough to do what God wants me to do." I write to all of you and ask, will you join me in loving God, following Christ, leading, being mighty young soldiers in God's army? Who is worthy of our praise today, right now? It is He who sits on the throne. Let's not let anyone look down on us because we are young, but set an example for the believers in speech, in life, in love, in faith, and in purity (1 Timothy 4:12).

CHAPTER 1

Growing Up

As a young boy, I rarely attended church in the religion of Catholicism, but when I did go, I was not interested. Every time I attended, I continued to lose interest until I decided that I wanted nothing to do with God. I grew up in Laredo, Texas, with a single mother and two sisters, whom my mother would encourage to go to church. When I was twelve years old, she started attending a Christian church without my sisters and me. One day I decided I would join her, and when I got there, I found out that the sermons were only in Spanish and I didn't understand them. Once again, I lost interest. Two years later, one of our neighbors invited my older sister to another Christian church, and when she came back, she said, "John, you need to come to this church; everyone was so nice, and it's in English!" So I thought I would visit and came to find their slogan very true: "One visit may change the way you think about church." It was the start of my journey with God that continues today. James Mendoza, the youth pastor then, walked up to me and asked for my name. He invited me to youth group, and I told him I would think about it. The only thing I really thought of was that I didn't want to join some cheesy group and participate in activities I had never done before, such as praying out loud in front of others. However, James didn't give up on me, or should I say, God.

February of 2000 came around, and it was Super Bowl time, which was a pretty big event on my calendar. James told me about the Super Bowl party that he was having for the youth, and free pizza and drinks would be provided. Yes, it was the free food that caught my attention! I gave it a shot and was amazed at how wrong I was about them being a cheesy group. I made new good friends and continued to connect with Pastor James. That same year, in late June, I found out that the youth would be taking a trip to a big conference called Challenge 2000 (a conference held every two years), which was being held in Indiana that particular year. I envisioned it as the perfect opportunity to get out of Texas and travel. When I asked if I could go, I was told that the cost for the conference was pretty high. In addition, the youth had spent all year fundraising for the trip. It was impossible to come up with a substantial amount of money in just two weeks, or so I thought. I remember a couple of nights before the trip, James, myself, and some others went to eat dinner at a Sonic drive-through and the conversation surrounded the big trip they were going on. I simply told myself, *Oh well, maybe the next time*. God had better plans and ideas for my life than just, "Oh well maybe next time."

The following night, I was at home watching TV when the phone rang. It was Pastor James. He asked if I was still interested in going to the conference, and I thought, sure, but how would I go? He explained that one of the students scheduled to go on the trip had discovered his grandfather had passed away. He wouldn't be able to make the trip, and there would be a vacancy for someone to go in his place. James said, "John, it's paid for, and all you have to do is pack." It was one of the greatest feelings I came across. That was one of the first times in my life that I felt like I needed to be somewhere. The next day, we were on our way to Challenge 2000 and the start of God revealing Himself to me in many ways. When we arrived at Purdue University, it had been a long drive and everyone was tired and just wanted to rest. As I looked at the schedule for the week, I noticed that the first rally was that same night. My negative attitude consumed me as I just wanted to go to my room and sleep. We went to the rally, and as I walked into the conference auditorium, hyped-up students were getting ready for something I had never seen before. As the music was playing, hands went up into the air and knees were on the ground, and I thought to myself, *What should I do? Should I do the same or what?*

That week, I experienced God in a way I never had before. When we got back from the trip, I made the decision to accept Jesus Christ as my Lord and Savior. I entered high school, but it was not long before I got caught up in the ways of this world—of course, high school world. Playing football, a dating relationship, and parties that were filled with drugs and alcohol were part of that world back in high school. By the grace of God, I was never involved with drugs, although I did drink on certain occasions. As time went by, I found every excuse not to attend youth group and slowly slipped away from having those godly people in my life. Time lapsed, and on April 15, 2003, I was the passenger in a horrific car accident. As I was lying in the hospital bed, the nurse was cleaning the cuts on my neck sustained from the crash. Apparently, I had a hole in my neck, and whatever had punctured it missed my breathing tube by an inch and a half. The nurse had told my mother that I was very lucky, but I knew deep down inside that it wasn't luck. I walked out of that hospital breathing, so I knew God still wanted me here for His purpose.

My last year in high school was a roller-coaster ride. I attended church regularly but only certain occasions with the youth group. I tried harder to be a better Christian; however, I still felt a little empty inside. During that year, I started to raise enough money to attend the Challenge conference. The time came around once again to load the bus and head to Salt Lake City, Utah, for Challenge 2004. On my way there, I got to meet new people and build friendships. In the midst of all the laughing and joking, it hit me hard: I hadn't had any fellowship with other believers, and I needed it. We arrived in Salt Lake City, checked into our rooms, and headed for the first rally of the week. As I walked into the room, I looked around at all the other students and listened to them get excited over what was to come. At that very moment, it was as if God spoke to me and said, "John, you remember this? Remember: four years earlier you walked into this same conference not knowing me, and it was then that I poured out my grace on you. Remember, John, who it was that you gave your life to, the one true living God who wants to have an everlasting relationship with you." The strong feeling ignited the need to start a personal relationship with God, and indeed I did.

On the way home from the conference, I was thinking to myself, *So that's it. I mean, it ends here.* It was my last year in the youth group and an overwhelming sense of emotion. *There has to be more fellowship and worship, and this experience cannot possibly end here,* I thought. Over the summer, I prayed about possibly helping out in the youth group as a middle school leader. In my opinion, it was an opportunity to pour back into the lives of younger students as older youth leaders had impacted my initial relationship when I was first introduced to this life. I began in the fall as the middle school coleader, and I have to be honest, I had no idea what I was doing. All I knew at that point was that I needed to be on time to youth leaders' meeting and follow through with my commitment to these adolescents. During that year, the college group, Campus Crusade for Christ, was having their weekly meetings at the local university. A friend I grew up with, who began in the youth group and was now affiliated with the college group, started calling and inviting me to the group. I knew they were meeting and hanging out, but I told myself that I was too busy to join them, so I always had to say no. It was the second to the last CRU night, and I decided that I would go check it out. It was awesome! They worshipped, played a cheesy game, and gave a message. It excited me, and I wanted to get to know these other college students better, so I started socializing with them regularly. Well CRU ended for that year (they didn't meet over the summer), and at that point I wanted to be involved in any way possible.

Over the next month and a half, I felt a tugging at my heart to ask the student leader how I could help out. Finally, one night I was praying before I went to bed, and the tugging had gotten so strong, I just said, "All right, God, I'll go ask, but I don't know what I'm going to be doing. But I trust you." The next morning, we had just gotten out of church, and I approached the leader and told her I wanted to get involved. I went on to tell her that I would like to start by taking the snacks to the Tuesday night meetings, and right there, she broke down and started crying and thanking God. She was overjoyed and thanked me as well.

After the crusade coleader thanked me, I have to admit, I was confused. I did not understand. The following week, I met with her and asked, "What was last week all about?"

She said, "John, I have been praying all summer for God to send me some help with the college group. I had been praying hard, and nothing was happening." This was the same amount of time that I had felt a tugging in my heart to look into the college ministry. She continued, "That morning, I had made the decision that I was going to throw in the towel, call it quits."

I said, "No, don't do that." I started my first year coleading the college ministry with two student leaders. We started meeting weekly on Thursday nights at the local university. It was the beginning of an amazing journey and a development of passion for aiding college students and the young generation. That year was the first time I even spoke in front of a group of people and gave a Bible study. I met many young people through the college ministry years. I encountered many challenges with people and events. Nevertheless, the bond and God-driven love that was created among such a unique group of people impacted many lives. These people who encouraged me as I began to lead the college ministry include Pete Saenz, Christie Ramos, Espie Soler, and Tony Herebert. For the next two and a half years, God would continue to grow all of us in our relationship with Him. Of course, we had our moments, but nothing broke through the love that God had given us for each other.

The Lord eventually led us down our own paths. I lead for the next two and a half years and then decided to step down as I was given the opportunity to serve as a deacon in the church. Danny took over as leader of the group for one year, which was his last year before graduating with a bachelor's degree. He would move on to be accepted to medical school in San Antonio, Texas. Back in 2007, Pastor James, who is now senior pastor of Vista Community Church in San Antonio, asked me to consider a youth/college pastor internship with Vista. I prayed for a good while. During that time, I was working a full-time job at a middle school and was still leading the college group. A year and a half passed after he asked me, and a vivid memory came to my mind one day as I was praying about this opportunity. Eight years earlier, I was saved under Pastor James's youth ministry. Throughout high school, I attended youth group on and off, and my relationship with Christ was weak. James never gave up on me. Every time I came, he reached out to me and did his best to pour into my life. At the beginning of my senior year of high school, I found out that James was leaving for seminary, and then to eventually plan a church in the San Antonio area. I thanked him for everything, and that day I told God, "If that guy ever does plant a church and he needs help, I will drop my things and go if you lead me down that direction." Eight years later, I was praying about this opportunity because Vista was looking for a youth minister. I simply told God, "I trust you. I will go."

I served as a deacon at Grace in Laredo for the first seven months of 2009. I then made the move up to San Antonio. I have now completed my eighteen months, and I believe the Lord has pointed me in another direction; "I am not ashamed of the gospel, because it is the power of God for the salvation of everyone who believes" (Romans 1:16). I don't know why God has chosen me to be a servant of His, but I know He has. If I could line up with the Apostle Paul when he said in 1 Timothy 1:15 that he is the worst of sinners, I would say the same. Praise God for His grace!

CHAPTER 2

Mighty Young Soldiers

I was introduced to this guy by the name of Pablo Monreal, who was enlisted in the National Guard. Now, Pablo was not a believer and had just come down to Laredo for the first time. He had no family or friends, only those who were stationed with him. Over a period of time, I had a chance to get to know Pablo, and the very first thing that I noticed was his self-disciplined attitude toward everything and everyone. When you talked to him, he would stare you straight in the eye with a serious look that I have to admit was very intimidating. But every time I spoke, no matter what I said, he always had a way of relating it to the army. He never complained or argued; moreover, he always kept a positive attitude. That's basically the same mentality God wants us to have. We wake up to a world of war in which our enemy seeks to defeat us. There are numerous battles filled with drugs, alcohol, sex outside of marriage, and addictions to pornography. There are small situations in which we tend to overlook when the enemy is at work. For example, a guy and a girl are in a dating relationship

9

and they have just come out of a movie, when they jump in the car and the guy asks, "So what else what do you want to do now?" The girl replies, "Well, it's kind of late, but I don't want to go home yet." Right then and there, the enemy will speak to the guy and say, "Drive her to a nice spot where you can park the car and just . . . talk. She would love it because it would be romantic." So the guy shares the idea that's on his mind, and before she responds, Satan will tell her, "Yeah, it would be beautiful: the night sky, only the two of you under the stars." Don't misunderstand me, there is nothing wrong with parks, night skies, and stars; on the contrary, it is the intention of the heart that is being targeted.

We think those small scenes in our lives are just part of life, and they may be, but don't forget that there is an enemy who plays a vital role. Now, just like a captain would not send his soldiers into battle without weapons, neither does God. For He is our ultimate commander-in-chief, who has provided everything we would need to fight these battles. Trust the armor that God has given us, which Paul speaks of in Ephesians 6:13-17. Satan has all kinds of tricks in the bag, and those tricks have been the same since the fall of man. I once read a quote that said, "One of the greatest tricks the devil ever pulled was convincing the world that he didn't exist." When you're in the midst of a struggle and you catch yourself saying, "I can't do this anymore," you are right. Only God can, and by relying on His strength daily, by receiving the faith that He gives us daily, and allowing His grace to pour down on you daily. You need to know that you do not wake up to this world of war on your own. You are not the only one struggling. For what soldier walks into a war on his own? Not one! But he walks in with his brothers who have his back. Which brother or sister has your back? Or whose back do you have? I have a brother in Christ, Danny Flores, who is there for me when I am struggling and when I simply need someone to talk to and pray with. But I don't mean any kind of talking, I mean on a whole different level. I can and have told Danny everything about me. In the same way, he has told me everything about himself as well. We hold each other accountable for our walk with Christ. We have agreed to allow each other to ask questions that most would consider personal. Confessing your sins to someone you trust is a sign of strength, not weakness. God is faithful in bringing healing: if we confess our sins, He is faithful and just, and will cleanse us from all unrighteousness (1 John 1:9). Fellow brothers and sisters, I know how hard it is to open up and tell someone about your deepest, darkest secrets, but know this: there is an Almighty God who is all-knowing; therefore your secrets are not as deep and dark as you think they are. In addition, I know you're afraid to be judged or looked down upon. For this reason, it is important to build a strong friendship and get to know the person that you will decide to confide in.

I got to know Danny for a year until we found ourselves sitting down, facing each other at a conference, ready to talk about something deep. We arrived at the Dallas Winter Conference in January 2006, and one of the guest speakers talked about how important it is to confess your sins to one another. He did not define confession as standing up in front of a group of people, but simply engaging with someone you trust. In the middle of the week, Danny asked me if we could talk when time was available to us. At this point, Danny and I knew nothing about each other. It was just the simple things, such as how old we were, how many are in the family, what his major was, and so on. So we got together, just the two of us, and I remember Danny saying, "John, I feel like I've got to do this, and I want to do this." Danny started confessing many sins he had committed. As he was talking, I could hear his voice cracking at some points. He was nervous, but something strong inside allowed him to do this. As I sat there, I just looked at him and saw the strength and the courage that it took for him to confess. After he did so, I could see the peace that God had put in Danny's life. Since then, we have been accountability partners and just recently made a life promise to each other: no matter where we're at or how old we get, we will make it a point to keep that connection, even if it means flying across the world. Like I said, who has your back, and whose back do you have?

Now, being a soldier means you're going to be involved in daily battles. I am specifically referring to the moment when your enemy is constantly looking for a way to destroy you. Satan has two main goals: first, he wants to take us to eternal condemnation with him, and second, he wants to make us ineffective for God in this world. If you have placed your faith in Christ, he has lost that battle. You cannot be eternally condemned, for it is written in John 5:24, "I tell you the truth; whoever hears my word and believes him who sent me has eternal life and will not be condemned; he has crossed over from death to life." His next and only objective is to try to make you ineffective for God. One thing we need to know first is that God does not need us, but in His love, He wants us. Unfortunately, you will not experience daily victories 100 percent of the time. Within some of those daily failures, you must leave room for humbleness, repentance, and experiencing God's loving hand of correction. Just like your biological father or guardian disciplines you, so will your Father in heaven. Hebrews 12:10 tells us that God disciplines us for our good, so that we may share in His holiness. It goes on to say that no discipline seems pleasant at the time, but it produces a harvest of righteousness.

I remember one time when I was back in the middle school youth group, I experienced God's loving hand of correction at the time, which at first was not pleasant but did produce righteousness. One youth night, James had us all sitting in a circle while he was wrapping up the night with his message, and I decided that it was a perfect time to be a clown and distract other students. James warned me once and politely asked me to stop, and I continued. James then asked me to leave the youth group for the night, and I walked out angry, thinking, *He's overreacting.* I did not go back for a couple of weeks until James and I clarified the situation. Even then, I still thought he overreacted, but God knew what He was doing. He was showing me that if I ever wanted to read and understand His word, if I ever wanted to gain respect, if I wanted Him to speak to my heart, then it was very important to be able to sit and listen to James when he was giving a message. You see, when you are in the presence of one who is sharing the truth of God's Word and you interrupt, you are really interrupting God. Satan was using everything he could to try to make James ineffective that night, but James did not let his guard down. In the summer of 2007, I was going through many trials of my own and I found myself crying out to God and at the same time asking myself, *What's wrong? What's wrong? I have never struggled like this.* It came to a point where I hit my knees and thought, *Man, if Pablo saw the way I was complaining, he would tell me to get up and be strong.* Right then I prayed and surrendered my struggles to God. It is okay to cry out to God, but when it is all said and done, He wants us to get up on our feet and get back into His formation, because we are mighty young soldiers in the only unstoppable army led by the victorious commander-in-chief.

CHAPTER 3

Shake Well before Use

I remember waking up Tuesday, April 15, 2003, and getting ready for school just like any other day. I was a junior in high school and went off on my usual routine, driving to John B. Alexander High. I walked into my first class, second, lunch, and by the time I knew it, school was out for the day. April 15 would turn out to be a day I would never forget. As my car pulled up to the driveway (I was the passenger), I took off my seatbelt about seventy-five feet away, thinking I was going to jump out of the car and go to the backyard, where some food was being cooked on the grill. The moment I took off my seatbelt, I heard the sound of the engine pick up fast. I looked at the speedometer and it read about fifty miles per hour. Then I looked forward and saw something in front: the car had crashed into the neighbor's tree, head on, and I went unconscious. I woke up to the smell of smoke, thinking the car was on fire. I looked to my left, and the driver was not in the driver's seat anymore. I told myself, "If I don't get out of here, I am going to burn." The car was smashed in, and the passenger door was jammed, so I had to crawl out through the driver's side. As I was crawling out, I could see that blood was falling onto the seats, but I had no idea where it was coming from. I stood up out of the car, and I could feel air passing in my neck. I put my hand on my neck below my chin, and when I let it go, blood just started spilling out, fast. My vision started to fade and I could no longer see straight anymore. Everyone who was in the back yard ran to the front as they heard the sound of the impact, and one person jumped in the bed of my truck and lifted my head, doing everything possible to keep me conscious.

The paramedics arrived at about nine thirty, put me on the stretcher, and stuck what felt like ten needles in me. We arrived at Doctors Hospital, and they immediately took me to the emergency room. They had called my mom and told her what had happened. She got there shortly after I arrived. The nurses came in and started cleaning the cuts below my chin and on my neck. They started talking about checking how deep the cut was. I could hear everything they were saying, but for some reason, I could not talk. The nurse told me that I had a hole in my neck, and they needed to check how deep it was, so they stuck a long cotton swab in the hole. The nurses looked at each other, then looked at my mom and told her that whatever punctured my neck had missed my breathing tube by an inch and a half. When I heard that, I had no idea how serious that was. It wasn't until my mother asked what they meant and the nurses told her that if someone punctures his breathing tube, his chances of surviving are very slim. Of course, my mom took that pretty hard and started tearing up. The nurses were trying to figure out why I was having a hard time talking, and took me to get some X-rays. They found that when I hit the windshield head-on, my jaw came loose. The doctor ordered me to stay in the hospital for about two days because I was feeling very weak and could not move much. But in those two days, many friends came to visit me and spoke some very encouraging words. One stood out in particular.

During that time, my home church in Laredo, Texas, had an associate pastor who came to visit me and asked me the question that would start my journey, my walk with Christ, and my personal relationship with God. Remember, I had placed my faith in Christ, but I knew nothing about what it meant to truly have a relationship with Him. He asked, "John, can I ask you a personal question?"

I said, "Yeah, I'm always up for personal questions; I ask them myself."

He asked, "John, if you had died in that car accident, do you know where you would have gone?"

To be honest, I did doubt where I was going. So I said, "I think heaven, but now that I think about it, I'm not too sure." From that time on, I needed to know, after accepting Christ as my savior two years earlier, was I going to spend the rest of eternity with God? It would be the initiation of the journey of life with Christ. I checked out of the hospital and I went straight to J. B. Alexander High School (I needed to pick up all the assignments I had missed while I was out). After stopping by some of my classes, I went to Mr. Aguilar's room—my English 3 teacher. Throughout the year, Mr. Aguilar taught me more than English; he taught me to pursue what I really wanted to do in life and to be successful at it. He succeeded by demonstrating it himself in all that he did.

As I knocked on his door, I opened it a little, and he said "John?" He interrupted his class lecture to come see how I was doing, which was one of the concerns for me at that time and I will never forget. He told me that he was going to see me after school that day. Time went by, and I had conversations with Pastor James and was assured that I had eternal life according to my faith in Christ. I even came across this verse that assures us "I write these things to you who believe in the name of the Son of God so that you may know that you have eternal life" (1 John 5:13).

Now, I would ask myself, "Why would did this happen to me? Why did God allow it?" I'm sure you have asked yourself the same questions. Scripture clearly tells us that we will not have a smooth ride in life. There will be bumps and curves along the way. But there is only one who can calm the storms in your life. "Consider it pure joy, my brothers, whenever you face trials of many kinds, because you know that the testing of your faith develops perseverance. Perseverance must finish its work so that you may be mature and complete not lacking anything" (James 1:2-4). James tells us here to consider it pure joy when you face trials. But what joy is there when you are in financial trouble? Or when you have been accused of doing something that you did not do? When you come home and find out that one of your family members has been diagnosed with a terminal illness? Most of the time, we see absolutely no joy in any trials that we are facing. But God tells us that there is joy to be found in the heart of these times. That joy comes from knowing that the result is a tremendous blessing if we keep our eyes on God.

Let's look at the perfect example that Christ demonstrated at the cross. Hebrews 12:2 reads, "Let us fix our eyes on Jesus, the author and perfecter of our faith, who for the joy set before him endured the cross, scorning its shame, and sat down at the right hand of the throne of God." What joy is there in knowing that you will be nailed to a cross? What joy? You and I could not see it. You and I could not even begin to comprehend it. Jesus found joy because He knew that in the end, God would work out everything for His good. Notice the first part of the verse, "Let us fix our eyes on Jesus." We are to keep our hearts and minds focused on God during any trials. It is then that we receive strength, encouragement, peace, and joy found in our perseverance. And perseverance must finish its work, so that you may be mature and complete, not lacking anything (James 1:4). Perseverance is one way God matures us in Him. It strengthens our faith and exposes our weaknesses, only to be handed over to Him. It is nothing more than a test, and when you have stood against it, there is a tremendous blessing waiting for you in the end. These are the things that must happen to us in order to be effective for God in this world. We cannot live in this life not having been strengthened by the mighty hand of God. You took tests and quizzes in elementary school all through to your present age. They were necessary to see if you were ready for what you were taught. God wants to use you. Remember, He doesn't need us for His work, but He wants us. Are you ready? It's a question we have all been asked at one point in our lives.

Allow me to take you into an illustration in the football world. It was the beginning of the summer of 2003, and I was getting ready for summer training for the upcoming football season (my senior year in high school). I knew I lacked in several areas. I needed speed, endurance, strength, weight, motivation, and heart. Had the coach asked me if I were ready for the upcoming season, my answer would have been a quick no. I ran sprints and long distance, pulled tires to gain speed, lifted weights for more strength, and continued to set my eyes on our goal, which gave me heart. The summer had passed and August was here. You know what that means: two-a-days. We woke up early and were at practice by 6:30 a.m. and on the field by 7:00 a.m. There was still a lot of work to be done, such as hitting drills, running the offensive and defensive plays, learning the proper techniques, and so on.

We hit hard, ran fast, endured the pain, but stood the test. No one dropped out! No one quit! In the minutes before the first game, our coach asked that famous question: are you ready? Our answer was a quick, "Yes, sir." After all the testing and perseverance, we were confident in our answer. You see, there is confidence and strength found in our God. Where there is our God, there also is our victory. Through Him we have the confidence to be well used by Him. He is the ultimate trainer—one who never loses, but has already gained all victory. His strengths are above all strengths. He equips us with everything we need to serve Him strong. Trust and allow Him to use you. Football players don't train to show up and sit on the bench. They want a piece of the action. In the same way the desire is in them, it should be in us. The desire should motivate us to want to tell others about God, to study His word, and to live obedient Christian lives. My prayer is that all of you will fix your eyes on Christ during your storms and struggles and know that God is equipping you for His work.

CHAPTER 4

In Speech

We all know the story about the sinking of the *Titanic*. The ship began its maiden voyage on April 10, 1912, from South Hampton, England, heading toward its destination, New York City. Just four days later, the temperatures dropped to near freezing, and the ship that once was advertised as designed to be unsinkable would go down in the middle of the Atlantic Ocean. Many warnings were made earlier in the day that icebergs lay in the path of the ship. At 11:40 p.m., lookout Fredrick Fleet sounded the bell three times and telephoned the bridge, exclaiming the famous quote, "Iceberg right ahead!" Officer Murdoch ordered the pilot of the ship to steer left, but it was too late. It struck the iceberg, and about two hours later, the ship went down, taking approximately twenty-two hundred souls into freezing waters of the Atlantic. You see, Officer Murdoch ordered the ship be put in reverse, which caused it to stop turning. If he simply would have kept steering left at full speed, it is said that the ship may have missed the iceberg. It is exactly what James tells us, "Take ships as an example. Although they are so large and driven by strong winds, they are steered by a very small rudder wherever the pilot wants to go. Likewise, the tongue is a small part of the body, but it makes great boasts" (James 3:4-5). Just like the pilot is in control of which direction he wants to steer, we too are in control of what we say. Let's dig out details.

When Paul said to be an example in speech, we have to think of the many different conversations we carry on daily. Let's take a dating relationship, for example. God calls all His children to be pure in every way, and that applies to our conversations as well. There are so many seductive words that will lead to lustful thoughts, and as a result, produce an act of impurity. When you speak to your significant other, what is the true meaning of your words? What is your purpose for saying them? Unmarried brothers and sisters, if you aren't sure if your words are seductive or impure, ask yourself, "Would I say this to Jesus?" These conversations not only apply to our significant others but our friends too. Brothers, the way we talk about women when they are not around can cause one of us to stumble. What is said to one another can generate thoughts that the enemy can easily grab a hold of. When we are hanging out with a fellow brother, we can get tempted to say, "Look at her. She's this or that." Such speech is in no way uplifting and encouraging to a friend who struggles with lust and impurity—or uplifting and encouraging at all!

Words of Encouragement

While chained in prison, the Apostle Paul wrote the letters of encouragement to churches from town to town and village to village. His words became the truth they needed to hear, whether they were on the right path or not. Let's take a look at the different ways Paul used to express his encouragement in words. In Galatians 1, Paul opens with honest feelings and expresses them through his words. Verse 6-7 says, "I am astonished that you are so quickly deserting the one who called you by the grace of Christ and are turning to a different gospel—which is really no gospel at all. Evidently some people are throwing you into confusion and are trying to pervert the gospel of Christ." Paul lets the people of Galatia know that it bothers him to see them deserting the gospel of Christ. He continues to express his concern that some are confused and that others are perverting the gospel. Their behavior was so evident; therefore, Paul saw the deep need to write a letter addressing these very things. Paul had a purpose for writing this letter, not to discourage but to encourage. When approaching someone about a situation you have a concern for, let them know how you feel. Don't beat around the bush, but let them know in a way that leads to words of encouragement on your behalf. Paul tells the people straight out that what they are following is completely false, and they need direction. He does so firmly, but in love! The Galatians are reminded that anyone who preaches a gospel other than Christ will be eternally condemned. Because of Paul's love for them, he goes even further in reminding them that what he preached to them was no lie. The gospel he received was a direct revelation from Jesus Christ. You can see here that Paul does not want to see one of them led astray by a false gospel.

Any truth that can be shared with someone who needs the encouragement, should be said. Brothers: whatever it takes! I remember walking into my friend's house one day and noticing that he was still down after a couple of weeks. I asked him if everything was okay, and his reply, with a low voice, was, "Yeah, man."

Right then and there, I expressed my deep concern for him. I told him straight out, "Hey, I need to talk to you. I have noticed that you have been like this for a while. Every time I see you, you're down and discouraged. What's going on? Is there any way I can help or pray for you?" He still insisted that he was okay. I said, "You know, that's fine, but the way you have isolated yourself from others, the way you show no care when we are having our Bible study is not only going to continue to affect your walk with Christ, but others as well because they care and love you too."

He then turned and looked at me with teary eyes and said, "John, I'm struggling with something." It was in that very moment that I knew I had to remind him of how I struggle to fight the good fight of the faith every day. I even went further and told him to ask me anything he wanted to know about my struggles if that would encourage him. Let me tell you that this brother of mine is not my accountability partner that I share and bring my sins out into the light with. But seeing the hurt in him, and knowing the love I had for him, I was more than willing to share anything if that's what it took. He broke down and confessed what he was struggling with. After doing so, he exhaled a breath of relief and allowed me to pray for him. This conversation led to him approaching me a couple of days later, asking me to hold him accountable to his struggle. That is exactly what Paul followed up on after expressing his concern. He told of his previous way of life. Galatians 1:13 reads: "For you have heard of my previous way of life in Judaism, how intensely I persecuted the Church of God and tried to destroy it." I believe Paul said this to remind the church at Galatia that he can relate to their current ways, but also to show that God called him to His ways, and they too were being called. Notice Paul talked about his own previous ways and no one else's. Talking about someone else's situations can lead to Satan's favorite conversations and our next topic, gossip.

James continues targeting the tongue in verses 7-8: "All kinds of animals, birds, reptiles and creatures of the sea are being tamed and have been tamed by man, but no man can tame the tongue. It is a restless evil, full of deadly poison." Mankind needs at least some form of communication to survive. With our words, we have the power to poison other minds anytime we speak. In our world today, gossip is completely restless; it knows no sleep. When there are a couple of Christians standing in a circle talking about who did what with whom, it is Satan's green light to use those words to devour the love and peace that we are called to have with one another. Every day, gossip is a hot battle of its own in our spiritual war. Our enemy has definitely made it easy to grab a hold of. As a matter of fact, he goes the through hard work by setting it up for you, and he has no problem doing so. Log on to websites; what sections do you usually find? You will come across those that are titled "celebrity gossip." Take your workplace, for example. It is very easy to walk into a little circle of gossip, whether you turn one way or the other. Satan will spice up the latest news right before your ears, and it will feel good to know about it. But what benefit is it to me if I know this information about this other person? What benefit is it to them? Many tight brother and sisterhood relationships have been loosened as a result of just sharing information that did not need to be shared. Now, there are exceptions. If you know someone is in danger of hurting himself or others, I encourage that you go talk to one of your spiritual leaders in the church who is in a position to take on the situation in a godly manner. That is because of your concern for them, not because of the pleasure of sharing what you know for no reason at all. If you have been hurt by someone, you need to tell him and not his close friends. If you feel like you need to confront someone in sin, confront him and not your parents or other relatives. We will discuss speaking and confronting others with love a little later.

Now, you may ask yourself, "How do I know what is being said is gossip, and how do I stop it before it goes any further?" I am going to use Pastor Tom Schmidt's three questions for this. When people come up to start talking about another person's situations, the first question you should ask is, "Why are you telling me this?" If they have answered legitimately, then ask, "How does telling me this benefit the other person?" If they have answered again, this last question should put a stop to it: "Have you told this person?" Exchange no further words with them, but rather, encourage them to bring these very words to the person's attention. Many times, gossip could sneak up in different forms. One way would be through prayer requests. Often, when we find out about something happening in someone's life, we ask around about the details and say, "So I can know how to pray for them?" using that as an excuse to know the details. Don't get me wrong: we are called to battle in prayer for one another daily, but God will make the details known to those who should know. For instance, if you know that your friend is going through a hard time and you want others to pray for him, you can simply say, "Hey, John, this person is going through a hard time. Can you please pray for him?" Notice that no details were made in the request, which leaves no room for gossip. It is just a pure heart to start praying.

Another method would be through our small group Bible studies. Satan will strive to take the focus away from teaching each other God's truth and head down a different road with, "Yeah and this person has done this or done that to me." I remember asking a person once, "How was your small group study tonight? What did you learn?" Their response was to tell me things that other people had done. If you are a small group leader, I encourage you to always keep in mind the focus of the night and do not allow the enemy to pull up a chair and join the conversation. Let those seats be taken by God's beloved children.

This Should Not Be

It is an indescribable feeling when we gather together and shout unto God with words of praise. For out of the heart come words. The sound of God's people lifting up one voice of praise is what we were made to create. Not only in church on Sundays, not only during the conferences, not only on the mission trips, not only in your small groups during the week, but always in our conversations, comments, and in the midst of our anger we shall shout unto God with words of praise. Notice I said shout on not shout at. But what happens when we walk out of those scenes and suddenly find our conversations full of curse words?

A couple of months ago, I was remembering my life before I gave it to Christ, and one area stood out in my mind. I had a mouth full of curse words growing up. In every conversation, I could remember how often these words would fly out of my mouth. Often these words were said in a conversation, and often they were said to hurt others. Not too long after accepting Jesus into my life, I started to feel something tugging at me inside after I would worship God through singing. I did not know what is was, but surely I started to feel guilty after saying a curse word or two. About a week after that, I was involved in a small Bible study, and they were in the book of James. He says in chapter 3 verses 9-10, "With the tongue we praise our Lord and Father, and with it we curse men, who have been made in God's likeness." Out of the same mouth comes praise and cursing. My brothers, this should not be. I read it, looked up, and it hit me. I said, "That's it: the Holy Spirit is at work in me." The Holy Spirit was lovingly convicting me. It was telling me, "Yes shout unto God with words of praise, but absolutely do not shout out curse words with that same mouth." He opened my eyes to what it looked like when I would curse. First, it was not glorifying to God. We could make the loudest shout to God, but if we are cursing Monday through Saturday, the shouts of praise don't matter. Our Holy God has thousands upon thousands of angels praising and singing about how holy He is. They worship in truth and with pure words. The Holy Spirit empowers us to worship day and night in the same way. Second, it was not uplifting and encouraging to other believers around me.

Since my walk with Christ was just beginning, I was hanging out with other young believers. When I would say a curse word, they thought they would do the same. It went hand in hand. Sometimes I would be the first to say one, and the others would follow. Other times, they would be the first, and I would follow. Then I thought, These are the guys that I learn God's Word with, gather together with, and worship through singing with, and immediately Paul's words came to my mind: "this should not be." I also was not being a good witness to nonbelievers. Some were not convinced that I had given my life to Christ, and they didn't care to do the same. Paul's right: the tongue is a deadly poison. The hard part was, I really wanted them to have a relationship with God as well. That night, after the Bible study, I went home and asked God to forgive me and change this part of my life. He indeed washed my mouth with His holy soap. Our God is a faithful God.

Watch Out

A good majority of us are fans of jokes, at least the innocent ones. Then again, we are also fans of making fun of each other, knowing that the other person will simply take a joke. As far as I could remember, when a friend and I were comfortable, we would joke and make fun of each other. These friends are my brothers in Christ who were also involved with me in our college group. Among us guys, we had a lot of laughs. Making fun of each other sometimes was just the norm for us. That would all change one night while we were at the Dallas Winter Conference held by Campus Crusade for Christ. In the middle of the week, after the night rally, some of us guys were hanging out in my hotel room. We were laughing, joking, and having a good time. At least that's what it seemed like, until one of the guys made a joke that belittled one of our friends. After the joke was said, he faked a smile and then took on a serious face. His eyes got watery, and the room went quiet. He started to say how every time one of us made fun of him, it would stir up negative emotions inside of him. It would bring back memories of his childhood when he was bullied around a lot by other kids. He said as long as he could remember, one of his biggest struggles was low self-esteem. Every time we made fun of him, it got lower until that night when he broke down in the room.

I immediately realized the pain we had caused him with our words. I apologized and thanked him for being brave in confronting us about how he felt. His humility broke down many barriers of pride in that room. You can imagine six or seven guys in a room, crying as they shared things from the heart. The picture might be funny, but the feeling was indescribable. That night, I saw God use my friend's humility to bring unity among us brothers in a whole new way. The next day, I was reading and I came across this verse in Galatians chapter 5: "If you keep on biting and devouring each other, watch out or you will be destroyed by each other." I thought to myself, the whole time we had been making fun of each other, unintentionally we were devouring our group. The unity was so far from the unity that God calls us to have with each other. Praise God for His Love in bringing back that unity. The way I see it, Satan was using what seemed like fun through good laughs to blind us to our ungodly speech.

CHAPTER 5

In Life

Setting an example for all the believers in life could be very hard for the young generation—or is it only as hard as we make it? Being young in the faith in this world today is tough, but God has said that we can get the job done. Sure, it can be intimidating when you have other believers who are older than you. The thought of leading a Bible study when someone older can do it can be scary. The feeling of leading a congregation in communion with other leaders of the church can make you sweat profusely. Then it gets harder. To obey God's commands and walk in His ways is tough. He never said it would be easy, but He did promise He would be within us every step of the way. Even if we fail ninety-nine times, He will pick us up a hundred. Again, the job can be done if you believe not so much in yourself, but believe the God in you. King Solomon did it.

In 1 Kings 3, we see how the Lord appears to Solomon in a dream and told Solomon to ask Him for anything he wanted. Solomon tells God of how he is young and does not know how to carry out his duties. Can you imagine being very young and governing a people that were too numerous to count, let alone governing the chosen people of God? How's that for a sweat? But trusting the Lord, Solomon asked for a discerning heart to govern the people. This pleased God, and the Lord granted Solomon's request. At a young age, Solomon demonstrated masculine qualities and was no longer intimidated. When we look at different stories of the Bible, God calls the young to lead in this world as well. For one day, Christ will come back for young and old. God has called the young to set examples wherever they go. To be an example is to mirror Christ. What does that look like? I believe it's living a transparent life. Our walk shall be blameless. Now don't get me wrong: we can't live a perfect life, but we can live forgiven. God called us out of a dark corner to walk in His wonderful light. If that means bringing a sin into the light by confessing it, so shall it be. That way, there is no room for darkness to reign in your life, only light. It is a hard thing to do.

As I mentioned in chapter two, I confess to my accountability partner and other mentors. Yes, questions do go through my mind, questions such as "What is he going to think of me?" or "Do I really want to do this?" In the end, though, after confession, God is always faithful. He brings healing and joy back into your heart. This way you are being an example, especially to yourself, knowing that God believes in you as well. You can look in the mirror and see a small reflection of Christ. Now my question to you is: do others see that reflection of Christ in you? One thing I always ask God is to give me the strength to serve Him in brokenness and humility, and not on my own strength and pride.

Submit to Authority

Being young, obviously, there are a lot of people around you who are older. Most likely, the leaders in your church and Bible studies are older than you. As the younger ones, God has asked us to respect older people in a very unique way, especially those who God has put in a position of leadership and authority. This has to start at home first, with your parents. Ephesians 6:1-3 says "Children, obey your parents in the Lord, for this is right. Honor your father and mother-which is the first commandment with a promise-that it may go well with you and that you may enjoy long life on the earth." I know a lot of times it seems impossible to do that. Some of us have parents who are never there. Some of you may have parents who might provoke you or are angry all the time. All through this, you ask yourself, "How is it possible to honor my parents if they don't have a bit of respect for me?" There was a time when my mother and I went through a long period of just yelling and arguing. It got to the point where I was thinking about moving out because of all the things that were being said. No matter how mad my mom was, I was very wrong on my end. In no way was I honoring my mother by yelling back or saying hurtful things. As I prayed, I knew that God wanted me to honor Him by going and apologizing sincerely and discussing the issue with understanding in order to improve our relationship. Then some of you fall into the category of your father leaving at an early age. You grow up and reflect back on the days when you looked up at the benches of your elementary events and would not see him there. You watch your mother struggle all these years to support you and any other siblings you have, and wonder why in the world he abandoned you. Then twenty-some years later, he starts calling more often and wants a closer relationship with you, and you have the choice to look at him with hatred or forgive him completely and respect him as your father.

We have to remember that no matter if our parents have been there or not, God chose them for His reason to be our parents. Our job is to honor God by honoring them. It shapes and sculpts your character so that you are more able to submit to the leaders in authority. "Obey your leaders and submit to their authority. They keep watch over you as men who must give an account. Obey them so that their work will be a joy, not a burden, for that would be of no advantage to you" (Hebrews 13:17). Notice it says they "keep watch over you." I have two amazing pastors who God has blessed me and others with. They do a great job of not dictating their authority over others just for the sake of it, but they seek God in watching over the flock that has been entrusted to them. What a burden it would be if I constantly questioned their authority in disobedience or I simply did not follow their guidance. I can testify that God has humbled me in so many ways by teaching me submission to these two pastors and other leaders in my church. I have found that the more you practice submission to the authority here, the more you find yourself seeking to submit to God. Another blessing I noticed was that as a Campus Crusade student leader for four years, I did not have trouble with other members of the group submitting to the authority of the student leaders. Yes, there were hard trials and conflicts, but I experienced joy in leading a group that God had entrusted to me.

There are other types of submissions that God calls us to, the harder ones. If you are attending school, your professors are in authority over you. Just recently, I began taking online classes, and I got off to a bumpy start with one of my professors. I was not agreeing with some of the material he was teaching, and it caused me to strongly object to that material. His response was that my objection was not part of that course and I should move on. I was angry at first, but the Lord reminded me that he is my professor and I ought to respect him.

Identity in Christ

When you're born, something very powerful is born with you: your identity. You weigh this many pounds, you have this much hair and this color of eyes. You are placed in that little plastic box so your family and friends can try and identify you through the window.

Years passed, and you entered middle school and started to develop your own identity. Maybe you were the one who everyone wanted to sit with at the lunch table because you knew how to make them laugh. You were the skipper who knew the places to "hide," or the cheater who knew how to cheat without getting caught. Then you entered high school, and you matured a little more and so did your identity. You hung out with a certain group and that's who you were, or at least that's how people identified you. You played a sport and you were a jock, or you were known simply as somebody's boyfriend or girlfriend. Let's take it up a notch. Maybe you were the one who people went to for drugs and you knew where the party was going to be. Well, I am telling you now that no matter who you were or what you did yesterday, God wants you to have an identity in Christ. This is exactly what God told the Apostle Paul on the way to Damascus. If you read early Acts, Saul (Paul) was a leader in the Sanhedrin and had enough authority to give approval to a believer's death. While the "religious" leaders and the Jews were stoning Stephen, guess who was there approving his death—Saul. Saul had one strong identity: he was the ambitious Christian persecutor. People from all around the region and towns knew who Saul was and what he was capable of doing. This was his protected identity until Christ met him as he was traveling to Damascus. On his way, Christ met him and told him what he must do. This was the beginning of a new identity in Christ for Saul.

Immediately after his conversion, Saul began to preach the gospel boldly, and people were asking, "Isn't this the man who persecuted?" Paul continued in this new identity until his death. He continued working hard at it. Paul traveled from town to town, preaching, loving, and teaching others about Christ. He went through persecution, times of near death, and trials before religious leaders. In the midst of it all, his attitude was, "I know that God has chosen me for this purpose, and there is no doubt of my newfound identity." That is who he was, and no one would take that away. You need to know that if you are a Christ believer, you have a newfound identity.

A couple of months ago, I was talking with a former high school teacher of mine, and he was telling me how he had used me as an example in the class. After mentioning my name, someone said, "Oh yeah, I know him. He's that church boy, right?" I told the teacher to tell him, "It's Jesus freak to you." I told myself, "Well I must be doing a little something right. I know now that God has chosen me for His reason, I don't understand why, but I do know." Do you? Do you know that for His reason, God has looked past all the filth, all the ugliness that we bring to the table, and has seen value in us? It is amazing to know that God has allowed our failed identity to be renewed in Christ Jesus. The chief of identity theft will one day be turned over to the Chief Judge. Love, learn, and walk boldly in your identity in Christ!

CHAPTER 6

In Love

One day I was asked by a friend, "John, how do you do it? How do you love God so strongly every day?"

I said, "You know, I fail God every day, but you just have to be head-over-heels in love with God." People, before you can do that, you have to know something—not understand, but know—God is head-over-heels in love with you. His love for us is incomprehensible, but you can know that God is love! His love and the love we know it as are nothing alike. His love is undying, everlasting, fulfilling, comforting, force-driving, good, compassionate, mind-blowing, compelling, and strong! You see, in the beginning, God created the heavens and the earth, and saw that it was good. He spoke light into existence, and saw that it was good. He created man, and this time saw that it was very good. I can just picture God creating us with much love and patience. I can just imagine God in the process of creating someone, and an angel coming up and asking, "Who are you creating now?" I see God replying, "Kaytlin. I am putting her little eyes and ears in place, and carefully sculpting her gorgeous smile."

In order to be an example to others, you need to allow the love of God to reign in and through you. Let it be evident! Being a leader in this area is vital. As a matter of fact, it is so vital that when asked, Jesus replied, "Love the Lord your God with all your heart, mind and strength, and love your neighbor as yourself." Loving God and loving others sums up everything in your Christian walk.

Back in 2006, I went on a summer project with Crusade for Christ to Fort Collins, Colorado, and I remember the night we had broken into small groups. The guest speaker, John, captured a great picture by a story he told. The story involved him and his former college roommate. He spoke of how his roommate was very messy and often wasn't there to pick up after himself. There were times where he did not wash his clothes and would wear them dirty. Then he would come home and find John picking up after his mess and would tell John not to do that and that he would do it on his own. This went on for quite some time, and after several times, John's roommate told him to please not do that anymore. John turned and said, "You know what, man, just let me love you! Let me serve you!" Right there, his roommate asked why, and John was able to lay out the gospel. It's not easy to always love! As a matter of fact, it's a hard thing a lot of the time. But if we are to follow every example of Christ and His teachings, loving others no matter what, no matter whom, it is what we shall do. Christ's journey was not just a walk to His victory over death, but was a journey of love and victory. He was already beaten and weak when He started His walk to the place of crucifixion. As He started walking, He fell once, but knowing how much you needed a savior, He got up. He fell again, but the love for you and your family got Him up again! Scripture declares this happened while we had our backs turned against Him. All while we engaged in every kind of evil deed! All while we denied Him! Yet while we were still sinners, Christ died for us (Romans 5:8). This, brothers and sisters, should compel us to love always.

There is only one thing that God has said for us to be in debt in, and that is love for others: "Let no debt remain outstanding, except the continuing debt to love one another" (Romans 13:8). Our love toward one another must not be of small portion or only sometimes, but must remain outstanding. We have to strive for it every day. We only care about the times that it's easy to love someone, but when we are around those who we consider hard to love, we don't like to deal with it. Fact is, a lot of those times, God uses certain people in our lives to teach us the real meaning of love. God has set a great example by loving His difficult children. Earlier, I mentioned that I went to Challenge 2000, and it was there that I heard one of the greatest testimonies of love and forgiveness. The Columbine shooting had just happened a year earlier, and the parents of one of the girls who was killed was there to share some powerful words with us that night. I remember vividly watching the father step up to the podium, with his wife right next to him. He began by saying how he was the father of this girl, and he started to talk about different parts of her life that brought smiles. This time, it was tears. You could clearly see hurt, pain, and anger. Just when I thought he was going to condemn the killers with words, he said something to the contrary: "I forgive them." My eyes popped wide open as I could not believe what I had just heard. Now you have to remember, I had not received Christ into my life at this time, so I remember asking myself, *How could he ever forgive someone like that? They are not worth forgiving.* The thought of someone doing the exact same thing to one of my family members just angered me. As I look back, there is only one thing that gave them the power to forgive these killers. It was the love of and for God! You can see the power of God's love that compels people to do things unheard of. Scripture declares that no one is righteous, not one person. That would mean that you and I are not worthy of being forgiven for the sins committed against our perfect and Holy Father. For those who come to believe in the Son, the same words are said: "I forgive them." Instead, the Father sees the blood of the Lamb that stands in our defense.

Love and What Is Right

There are times when we are put into situations where we have a great opportunity to stand up for what is right and love someone, but we are held back by the people who are involved in the situation—or simply by fear. This should never be the case! Always stand up for what is right no matter what. Take Rueben's example; in Genesis 37, Rueben found out what his brothers wanted to do with Joseph, and immediately, he recognized the opportunity to love his brother. Even further, he recognized that their plan to get rid of Joseph was simply wrong. Just because they were brothers, he didn't say to himself, "I'll just stay out of this or go along with it," but rather, he devised a plan to help get Joseph back to their father. Even though Joseph was eventually sold, it was the condition of Rueben's heart that set the example. It was with sincere love for his brother that he tried to rescue him. Fellow believers are young men and women of integrity who chose to love someone despite who is involved. When the opportunity comes for you to join in on things that are dishonoring to God, and you choose not to, let your reasons be not only to protect your identity in Christ but simply because of your sincere love for God.

Toward the Family

One of my biggest struggles growing up was having a very bad temper. My fuse was pretty short. If you were a friend and an argument broke out, I would skip the argument and use fists. Obviously, this bad temper carried into my home, where I lived with nothing but ladies. Even though I loved them and they loved me, there were many times when they were intimidated by me. I wanted things done my way, and I used my temper and intimidation to get there. It caused a lot of hurt feelings and scars, but praise God, He turned it around. After I asked Christ into my life, I noticed that was one of the first struggles God dealt with. My eyes were opened, and I saw the hurt I had caused my family. Of course, I asked God and them to forgive me. From that moment on, I pursued God's counsel, through His people, in getting disciplined in this area. I can say now God has lengthened my fuse tremendously, although it is a daily battle. But it is a battle worth fighting, because these ladies I live with are the people God placed in my life as my biological family, and I do want them to know the love I have for them.

Again, it is not always easy; there will be those family members who are tough to love. You might be in that situation where your parents favor another sibling over you. Are members of your family being divided over a religious or political idea and you're stuck in the middle? Or maybe you are constantly picked on because of your faith. The bottom line is, you have a choice: love or not. Loving in these hard situations can simply mean being patient and diligent in prayer. Of course, there are times when these people need to be addressed firmly, but out of love. Something a lot of us need to recheck is that whole idea that Mom and Dad being around us when we are with friends is embarrassing. Sometimes they can do things that are a little strange, but remember, they put up with all our embarrassing moments growing up. This love that God speaks of is not one of telling your parents, "I love you," at home only, but around your friends too. Let them see God's love shine through you by letting them know they are appreciated, either by words or actions.

The Tough Ones

There have been many times in my Christian walk when God has brought people who are tough to love into my life. I'm sure you know what I am talking about. You and I can both make a list of people who just made it absolutely hard to be around them, much less love them. At the same time, God has placed you and me in someone else's life when it was hard for them to love us. It goes both ways. I don't always stop and think that I might be making it hard for a certain person to love me. We are all the tough ones. That is why Christ said to love our neighbors, not just our family—not just the friendly or easy ones, but the tough ones as well. Jesus knew from the very beginning that Judas was going to betray Him, yet the whole time they spent together, Jesus loved him.

John chapter 13 records the night Jesus showed His disciples the full extent of His love. It was just before the Passover feast, and the devil had already prompted Judas to betray Jesus. Knowing that, Jesus got up and began to wash His disciples' feet. Imagine, Jesus on His knees. He comes to Andrew and washes his feet. Then he comes to James, and then John, Philip, and finally to Judas. I wonder what was going through Jesus' mind as He looked into the eyes of His betrayer. Did He say, "I will not wash his feet," or, "Forget him; he is not worthy"? I believe not. Having previously told Peter that not everyone was clean, Jesus continued on His knees and washed Judas's feet while demonstrating the full extent of His love. Jesus tells them to go out and do the same (John 13:1-13). He tells us to not only read about His great example or think about His great example, but to go out and live it as well. Love not only the easy, but the tough.

The Rest

In June of 2008, I was boarding a plane that was headed to Nicaragua, along with eight other members from my church. I was going on my first oversees mission trip, and all I could think about was how cool it was to be able to serve God oversees. That excitement turned into something a lot deeper and real as we walked out of the Nicaragua airport and into our shuttle. The excitement, of course, was still there, but a thought crossed my mind. I asked myself why I was really there as I looked out the shuttle windows and saw life on this part of earth. The words hit me, "You are not loving completely until you're loving the rest." I saw a lifestyle that was very different from mine. God brought to my mind a list of blessings I had back home. I told myself, *The only important thing I have to offer these people is the message of the love of God*, and I believe we did to the best of our ability. Loving those people, whose concerns are not what are they doing tonight for fun, but where tonight's meal is coming from, was one of the most fulfilling events of my life. I have heard it said, "Why go overseas when the need is in your backyard?" If God's love extends even to the remote parts of the earth, the real question is, why not? If He provides the way for you to go to the farthest parts of the earth to carry His love, why not? Brothers and sisters, we are not loving completely until we are loving the rest.

The Apostle Paul went from town to town, country to country, and people to people. Of course, work hard in your backyard as well. We can start by obeying the Master's command when He says, "Go."

CHAPTER 7

In Faith

C had and Keri McCartney made their way to their regular
doctor's check up for baby Macie, not expecting the news
that awaited them. Twenty-three weeks into the pregnancy,
the ultrasound revealed a test for Chad and Keri. A tumor the
size of a grapefruit had formed on Macie's tailbone, and it was
stealing blood away from her. It was a rare and fatal condition,
striking one in thirty-five thousand babies. "At that point, we
didn't know—we didn't know what was going to happen," Keri
said. "We just felt all alone. Who will take us . . . who will help
us through this?" They contacted doctors who could attempt to
take Macie partially out of Keri's womb and remove the tumor.
Either way, Macie's odds of survival were less than 10 percent. I
remember sitting in the congregation when Pastor Chad shared
their situation and asked us to join them in prayer. After seeking
God and the counsel of their closest friends, they decided to go
through with the surgery. We have the opportunity to set an
example in faith on a daily basis, and why? We are faced with

decisions and situations that will expose where our faith is being placed.

Respond

"Be wise in the way you act toward outsiders; make the most of every opportunity," Colossians 4:5 tells us. This is a key verse that helps me to respond to every situation in reflectance to my faith. Of course, I don't always respond this way. This verse is telling us to be wise with our actions in every situation—not only in the friendly ones, but in the tough ones as well. Often, we don't realize the power of the type of response we give to others because of our faith. That spirit calls for peace, humility, humbleness, and love no matter what. Let's say you walk into a Starbucks, and at the counter you order a venti passion tea, and the employee talks to you in a rude way for whatever reason. He even goes as far as handing you your change back harshly. *You're thinking, Okay, time to confront this person, and I'm going to do it how I want.* But what you don't know is the worker to the right of this rude employee has just become a Christian, and he was just witnessing to another in the back. To his left is one who practices another religion, and right behind him, running the drive-through, is one who does not believe there is such love anymore among humanity. All eyes are on you; how do you respond? Let's take the negative route. You responded in the same way this employee treated you. In response to Colossians 4:5, it was not a wise decision. And you definitely did not make the most of that opportunity to witness to this employee in the most powerful way: loving others as Christ has loved you. You had the chance to say, "Hey, I don't know if you have had a bad day or something went terribly wrong, but I'd love to pray for you if you let me." It is the chance to show someone the power of Christ's love for him. Man, as I write this, all I think about is the many times that I failed and responded in a negative way. The chance to have a good conversation about Christianity with the employee who practices another religion has just plunged. The employee running the drive-through is now really convinced people can't love each other these days, so how can God love him? And of course, you did not take the opportunity to be an example to the new believer.

Now let's respond according to the faith we hold. The employee could possibly take you up on that prayer offer, and a seed is planted. The door is wide open for you to possibly have a peaceful conversation with the employee who practices another faith. The one running the drive-through is now thinking twice about our love toward each other, and the new believer has just seen an example and is ready to go out and do. Our response, either way, has much more of an impact than we can see. This, brothers and sisters, is the power of the Spirit of God that lives within us.

Now our faith goes through pop quizzes and longer, harder exams. We usually walk through the pop quizzes, but it's when the exam comes that our faith needs to remain and be even stronger. Sometimes we find ourselves crawling through the exam in our faith. Whether walking or crawling, let our faith remain and remain evident. At one point, I was crawling, literally!

On November 22, 2009, Thanksgiving Day started a little different than the previous years. This time, I woke up and stayed in that morning because I had retired from playing in the local Turkey Bowl. I did my part to help out in the kitchen (something I hadn't really done before), and for the first time, it was just my mother, younger sister (fifteen years old at the time), and myself. We ate at about one o'clock, took our nap, and then probably ate some more. It was then that I decided to make plans to go watch a movie. I remember getting ready. Mom was cleaning her room, and Kim was still napping in the other room. I walked to the kitchen, grabbed the car keys, and then the home phone rang. I stood there, trying to listen to who it could be as Mom was talking on the phone in her room. Mom then yelled for me, and I ran over to her. As I picked up the phone that had been dropped on the floor, I heard a young girl's voice say, "John, I'm just calling to tell you that Kimberlee is pregnant and you all should know. I'm just concerned for her health and safety." That was the first time in my life I felt like my heart stopped beating as it suddenly made sense why Mom was banging on Kimberlee's door, telling her to open it. I hung up the phone, ran to Kimberlee, and asked if it was true. Only one word came out of her mouth as she laid there, scared: yes. Mom was yelling and crying in the hallway, and I had no chance to fall to my own knees because I was doing my very best to hold her up. It was hard, so I called up Pastor Tom and Holly. Tom is like my dad, and he knows when something is wrong by the sound of my voice.

They came immediately and did their best to calm us down. At this point, I had not had a chance to break down myself, so they mainly helped my mom. As they were sitting there, I walked outside, made the couple of steps to the front lawn, and then fell. I fell all the way down to my stomach as I was crying like I had never cried before. I kept trying to pull myself up, but I found myself only reaching to my knees. It was here that I was yelling out to God, knowing that the only thing I had left to show was my faith in Him, if it was still there. Then I remembered the words I often tell God: "I will worship you hard when things are going good, and I will worship you even harder when things are going bad." My exam: "Do I still believe God is in control of everything no matter what?" God provided the necessary strength for me to remain strong in the faith and be an example to others as they have done for me. I now have two beautiful nieces: baby Kaylee, by my older sister Gina, and baby Kaytlin, by Kimberlee.

Service in the Faith

Once we accept Christ into our lives, the deal is sealed with a powerful deposit: the Holy Spirit. He empowers us for service. Use the gifts that He has given you to serve and bring glory to God. You are not too young to be up there preaching the Word of God if you have been properly mentored and trained. You are not too young to lead a group in holy worship through music. You are not too young to go out and evangelize as if Christ was coming back tonight. You are not too young! The body of Christ is made up of young and old. It should be our desire to put ourselves out there and allow God to use us how He chooses. Every morning when I pray, I tell God, "I have nothing to offer you but myself, and I am thankful that you still want me and have allowed me to be a part of your plan. God, all I want is a piece of the action on the field, and if possible, may I be a starter." With your heart in the right with God, seek how you can serve in order to bring glory to God. That's what it's all about: bringing glory to Him in everything we do. If you eat, bring glory to God. If you talk, bring glory to God. When you serve, serve to bring glory to God.

Baby Macie Continued

For the next ten weeks, Chad and Keri continued to pray for the health and healing of baby Macie. I believe God honored their prayers! On May 3, 2008, baby Macie was born, and when we found out, it brought immediate tears to my eyes. We all thanked God that day. I remember sitting in my living room with family when we heard the news. The next day, I got into my truck and headed on my usual route to work as I prayed my morning prayers. I continued to thank God for the display of faith by Chad and Keri. Then the words hit me, and it was as if God said, "Yeah, the guy walked on water!" After all this time, even after Peter took those steps and literally walked on water, we could do the same today in a spiritual sense by displaying our faith in God.

The thought blew my mind so much that I picked up my phone, with tears in my eyes, and called Chad. He answered, "What's going on, John?" and I replied, "Man, you walked on water." They were scared, and all they had was to simply trust God and accept the outcome. I know that had the outcome been different for Macie, Chad and Keri would have still worshiped God. Faith is not trusting God for a good outcome, but rather trusting God no matter the outcome. As young believers, we have the ability to display faith in mighty ways. Are we seizing those opportunities? If we knew the outcome of every situation, where would faith come in? What we can be certain of is that God is already in tomorrow, and He knows all things. Look for opportunities to allow your faith to be evident. If you're driving down the road and you see someone trying to push his car, stop and help if you can (of course, use discretion in every situation). If you see an elderly person trying to push her grocery basket, offer to help. In your prayers, ask God to give you these opportunities. Desire them! In all things, let your faith be evident for the glory of God. Walk on water!

CHAPTER 8

In Purity

We have to be in constant pursuit of God in different ways at all times! Every time I get the opportunity to share a message with young people, I will almost always teach on this topic. What about the constant pursuit of purity? No one is exempt from this command by God, certainly not me! All of a sudden it's okay to have sex outside of marriage. Guys, all of a sudden, it's okay to give girls provocative compliments. Girls, all of a sudden, it's okay to be flattered by these compliments. Then we try to justify it all by saying, "I was just joking," or "It's not like that." Then what is it like? What we don't realize is that our speech is just as powerful as our actions. What we don't see is that even when we're "just playing," these compliments have opened up doors that God has clearly said to keep closed. God is not trying to rob us of anything; on the contrary, He is holding us for a multitude of blessings that He wants us to have at the appropriate time. I have failed in this area in the past, and every time I have gone through the consequences, God has taught me the same thing: "John, this is why I say keep these doors closed. Keep them closed." God has asked us to use the parts of our body as instruments of righteousness and not wickedness (Romans 6:13). This includes our tongue (making provocative compliments); it is a part of the body and it should be offered as an instrument of righteousness as well.

If you back up, in verse 12 of Romans 6, it states, "Therefore, do not let sin reign in your mortal body so that you obey its evil desires." This is a tough area in our lives to avoid sin because God created sex in all its fullness and for us to enjoy in the appropriate way. It is man who has perverted it! We are not slaves to sin (through faith in Christ), and it is no longer our master. Rather, we are slaves to righteousness, because we are under God's grace. Think for a moment. What was this area of your life like before Christ? If you gave the parts of your body over to ever-increasing wickedness and impurity, through Christ you are forgiven! Now, make it a conscious point to give your body over to ever-increasing righteousness and purity. We often walk this Christian life without even thinking about how important this is to God and how it should be important to us as well. We walk around thinking of the things that are important to others. "My boss needs me to get this done today so I need to get it done." "Mom needs me to run this errand." "I need to go to my significant other's event to provide support." Yes, these are all important, but it's at the end of the day, when we are getting ready for bed that we say, "Oh yeah, God, I forgot to try hard here or there. I didn't pray when I was being tempted earlier. God, I'm sorry I missed our date today. I didn't meet with you." We go through the whole day not thinking of what's important to the God who thinks of us. It is God who opens your eyes every morning and keeps that breath of life flowing in and out of your lungs. By Him, you were able to get to the end of the day. For what man can do anything on his own? We are able to love God in this way because He first loved us. Having saved us in His grace, He then shared with us the things that are important to Him through His Word: good things and bad things. If I claim to follow the one true God, Creator of the heavens and the earth, lover and redeemer of my soul, then the things that are important to Him should be important to me. We have nothing to offer God but ourselves!

Now God does not only ask us to abstain from sex outside of marriage, but also to not have a hint of sexual immorality among us, because it is improper for God's holy people (Ephesians 5:3). Improper for who? It is improper for God's holy people. We are told to be holy as God is holy (1 Peter 1:16). So what does it mean to be holy? Being holy is simply being set apart for God and having a reason for it. It is because God Himself is set apart from all sin and evil. It is one of His perfect characteristics. Being holy as God is holy is being set apart from this world and its evil deeds. I'm going to share an illustration that helps me set myself apart for God—of course, there are times when I fail—and hopefully it will help you too. When you set yourself apart from the world, set yourself apart not vertically but horizontally.

When you set yourself apart vertically, you are intentionally or unintentionally setting yourself to the very standard of God. It is a perfect standard that no one can hold to but God Himself. Scripture makes it very clear that all have fallen short of God's standard (Romans 3:23) and only He sits on a perfect throne. God knows our imperfectness. He knows our sinful nature and finite minds. He is not asking us to hold His standard. Also, when you set yourself apart vertically, you set yourself above the world, leaving room for possible pride or conceitedness to root in you. This is that "Oh I am a Christian, and I am better than you or smarter than you" attitude, when clearly we are Christians because of everything God has done and nothing we have done. If it wasn't for God, we who know the Truth would be nothing. If we are above the world, then we cannot relate or bear witness to nonbelievers when Christ has commanded us to do so. Rather, set yourself apart horizontally. When you do this, you set yourself apart from the world and are under God's authority, under His shadow, under His wings. You are allowing Him to conform you more to His image while you are on the same level of the world, which you can still relate to. You are set apart yet still able to relate and bear witness to the world.

Every now and then, I get invited to a non-Christian friend's house to watch a boxing match or some event with other non-Christians, and occasionally, I go. I take these times to associate with them and do my best to witness to them. I don't talk or act in some of the ways that they do; but yet, I still associate with them. If I didn't just because I was a Christian, I'd be saying, "No, because I am a Christian I am better than you." Christ ate and sat with sinners, yet he didn't act or talk like them. He bore witness and shed light into these people's lives all while he was set apart for the Father. Set yourself apart, not vertically but horizontally.

Some of these hints of sexual immorality include what we are looking at on a daily basis. Sad to say, I was introduced to pornography at an early age. I can remember many childhood moments, and some vividly. I was playing Cops and Robbers outside with other kids from our apartment complex, and I ran into my friend's two-story apartment. His parents were at work, and only his older brother was home. This older brother called us upstairs, and it was there that I was exposed to pornography. I was in the third grade! I remember what I saw, and those images stayed burned in my mind for a long time. Those memories often had an effect on the way I viewed girls until the day I met Christ and He transformed my mind and life. I now became aware of how dishonoring it is to God to view such scenes. What we view does have an effect on our mind and thoughts. Christ said, "Anyone who looks at a woman lustfully has committed adultery with her in his heart" (Matthew 5:28). He wants us to keep a pure view. Cut the cord with anything that is making you stumble in this area. Maybe it's reanalyzing how much time you spend on the computer or when you get on it. Maybe for some, it's cutting the conversation short with someone who speaks lustfully. Whatever it is that's making it harder, cut the cord and ask God to help you see others through His eyes and not your own. Guys, make it an effort to view the ladies, in the name of Christ, for what they truly are: God's creation, made in His image. Any kind of impurity has an impact on our relationship with God. It causes interruption within the relationship as it dishonors God.

We often don't realize that even in these small things, we grieve the heart of God. Proverbs 6:18 says, "Feet that are quick to rush into evil"—this is one of the seven things that are detestable to God. As I read over this proverb, "feet that are quick to rush into evil" struck me hard. I remembered so many times when my feet were quick to rush into evil, and willingly too. God is telling us that He knows we are going to sin, but at least put up a fight. Don't just take joy in falling into temptation when it comes. Don't say, "It's just too hard, I might as well take part in the action." Unfortunately, we will not be 100 percent victorious in resisting temptation in this life, but He does wants us to fight hard in the midst of temptation.

I could not imagine any boxer who has gone through months of training stepping in the ring only to tell the opponent, "Your punching bag has arrived; jab me." Of course not. He is going to put up a fight. There are times when he will win and times when he will lose. But whether he wins or loses, at least he put up a fight. It should be our desire to obey God's Word in living a pure life and fight temptation with all our might. In keeping a pure view, we should also strive to keep a pure mind. Guys, what is going through our minds as we look at ladies? If we are constantly thinking impure thoughts, we need to ask God to renew our minds, as Paul tells us in Romans 12:2. Ask God to help you see the world through His eyes, which are completely pure. This comes with the reading of, studying of, and obedience to God's Word. It comes with being faithful in prayer (Romans 12:12). God is completely aware of how our minds function and how they can wander off. At the same time, He has told us that we have the ability to not think of the deeds of darkness and how to gratify the desires of the sinful nature (Romans 13:14). If we are to live pure lives for the glory of God, we need to stay out of the line of fire.

Here's a fictional story for you that does really happen on a daily basis. There was this guy who took a girl out on a date. They had a nice, romantic dinner, probably at Carino's, went to see a chick flick, and then drove off to a secluded area. They started talking about the family, problems, and stress, and then the conversation shifted to "better things." The next thing they knew, they had climbed into the backseat and their clothes came off. This is the part in the story where the guy says, "And then I got tempted." Whoa, back up there, buddy. You drove to a park with no one around late at night, talked, hopped into the backseat, took off your clothes, and then you got tempted? When did he actually put himself in the line of fire? You may say you are good enough, strong enough to place yourself there without falling into temptation. There may have been times where you did put yourself in such a situation and you did not give in. Praise God! But sometimes we start to think that we are above the potential to sin. There is no one righteous—no, not one (Romans 3:10). It seems logical to just stay out of these lines of fire. Some may ask, "Well, what are the boundaries with my girlfriend or boyfriend?" Second Timothy 5:1-2 says, "Treat younger men as brothers, older women as mothers, and younger women as sisters, with absolute purity." God has said, "Absolute."

Now what if you have engaged in sexual immorality or are caught up in it right now? I am going to use the story of the woman who was caught in adultery and brought before Jesus by the Pharisees in John chapter 8 to answer this question. Jesus asked the woman, "Where are they? Has no one condemned you?"

"No one, sir," she said.

"Then neither do I condemn you," Jesus declared. No one on this earth has authority to condemn you but God Himself. If you have placed your faith and trust in Jesus Christ for the forgiveness of your sins, and have asked him to be Lord over your life, you are a child of God and are not condemned, for "there is now no condemnation for those who are in Christ Jesus" (Romans 8:1). With this comes application. Christ told her to "go now and leave your life of sin." He is telling you the very same thing. "Go now and leave your life of sin." These are Jesus words to you today.

A couple of years ago, I met a college student who was so passionate in wanting to know more about his Savior. He came to our weekly Bible studies and showed up every Sunday for service. He was just craving a daily relationship with God. Then one day, he did not show up to our college Bible study. Then another week went by, and so forth. He even stopped coming Sunday mornings. After some time, I finally gave a call to this person and said, "Hey, I was just calling to see if you were all right. Is everything okay?"

He said, "No, John, everything is not okay. I've been struggling with this impure relationship, and I'm too ashamed to show up to college night. I'm too ashamed to face God on Sunday mornings." A lot of you are struggling with the same thing. You are drowning in a sin in this area of your life, and you feel like you are in too deep to get out. You also feel like you can't approach God. Let me tell you, it doesn't matter how deep you have gotten. It doesn't matter how far you have stepped away from where you need to be. It doesn't matter how long your back has been turned from God: He's waiting for you! From my personal experience, I can tell you, the moment you turn back to God, you will receive not a finger pointing back at you, but arms wide open. He will restore you to a right relationship with Him, gently. That's not to say there won't be any consequences, but there will be a loving hand of correction and acceptance. But He won't do this until you acknowledge your need for Him. He is not going to rush into your heart or try to break down any doors by force. You have to acknowledge your need for Him. There is no room for shame. That is what the cross is all about. Jesus stepped out of the glory of heaven to take on our past, present, and future sins so that we don't have to bear any shame in facing God. Jesus stands in my defense and in yours. Turn back to God! Lay your struggle at the cross and allow God to overpower you with His love and grace. That's who He is. That's what He does best.

CHAPTER 9

Obey Your Thirst

What does it mean to thirst after God? What does it look like to have our soul quenched by the Living Water? In June of 2009, I went on a mission trip to Nicaragua with my home church. It was the second time we made this trip (we had done it the previous year as well), and our objective this time was to help remodel an existing church. We arrived at the church work site, and I remember Pastor Tom saying to all of us, "You guys, just reminding you to drink plenty of water and stay hydrated." It was something he had enforced last year, and he was definitely enforcing it again.

So we told ourselves, "Okay, drink our water, stay hydrated, got it." We all went off to our assigned places, and I was at the front of the church. Now, there was a metal gate in front of the church, and I was supposed to brush off the all the dirt and rust that was on the metal so it could be painted over.

So there I am, brushing along and talking to others, when Pastor Tom stopped by and said, "John, have you taken a break?"

JOHN E. BARBA

A good two hours had already gone by and I had not taken a break, so I said no. Then he said, "Well go take a break, drink some water."

I thought to myself, *Man, he didn't even ask if I was tired or thirsty.* I was on a roll, I had finished parts of the gate, and I just didn't want to stop. But when I really thought about it, I knew I could use a break and some water. After I took my first drink, I realized how thirsty I was. I realized how dry my mouth was. Let me ask you a question: are you thirsty? I don't mean is your mouth dry, but is your soul dry? This world that we live in is a dry and weary land, and we as Christians should be thirsty. Not thirsty after the things of this world but after the things of God. Not only should we have a thirst for God, but we should be having that thirst quenched.

Some of you know what I'm talking about. You're physically thirsty, and you're thinking, *Which drink would hit the spot?* Then you do whatever it takes to get your hands on that drink. When you take your first sip, what do you do? You go, "Ahhhh." It is the same thing spiritually. You were praying for someone or something, and God answered your prayer or God did an amazing thing in your life and quenched your thirst, and you just want to say, "Ahhhh."

I am going to take you through a Psalm where we see David and his thirst for God. Now at this point, David is in the desert of Judah because King Saul is on the pursuit to take his life. Even in this extreme time of David's life, we see him expressing his need for God. Psalm 63:1 says, "O God, you are my God, earnestly I seek you; my soul thirsts for you, my body longs for you, in a dry and weary land where there is no water." First, David acknowledges not only that God is God, but that He is David's God; he says, "O God, you are my God." David then takes it deeper and expresses his constant pursuit of God. He says, "Earnestly I seek you." Then David digs deep into his very being, and says, "My soul thirsts for you, my body longs for you." You see, David is aware of his environment. Although he is in a dry and weary land, and it's hot and his mouth is dry, he says, "God, I am thirsty for you. Water sounds so good right now, but I know you are so much bigger and you have so much more to offer. I want you!" The enemy knows that people are thirsty. Even more, he knows that Christians are thirsty, and he will work overtime to meet that thirst with the things of this world. As Christ's followers, we need to stop and say, "God, the things of this world sound so good right now, and the truth is, many a time I want them, but you know what? I want you more. I want you more, because I know you are so much bigger and you have so much more to offer."

I've put together a simple definition of what it means to thirst after God. It can be defined as the constant pursuit of God's heart. Not a weekly or bi-weekly or even a monthly pursuit, but a constant pursuit. Think of two officers who get a call on their radio about a suspect in a stolen vehicle, and they respond because they are nearby. Now they are pursuing the stolen car, and their adrenalin is rushing, their hearts are pumping fast. At this point, what two officers in their right mind would pull over for anything? Who in their right mind would say, "Partner, stop at that gas station. I'm thirsty," or "Let's get a quick bite in a drive-through and then try to catch up"? No, they are going, and nothing is stopping them until the end.

One way you can pursue God is through obedience. Where does God have you in life right now? What opportunities has He given you to obey Him? You have heard it said, "Obey your parents." Ask yourself why. It is because when you obey your parents and you do it with a good heart and attitude, you can honestly say, "God, this is one way I am pursuing you." It's usually obeying them in the little things that often don't seem important, such as washing the dishes or taking out the trash. You see, it's not so much the action of taking out the trash or washing the dishes that God is concerned with. It is the condition of your heart at the time you were doing those things that He is looking at. When He sees that you did these things with a good and joyful heart, He will see that, at a young age, you are pursuing Him.

What does your communication with your parents look like? Do you have one of those mind-sets where it is okay to talk to them however you want, even if it means talking to them in a bad way just to get your point across? Granted, not all parents are easy to talk to. Not all of them listen. Not all of them may seem to understand. In the end, though, God has placed them as the authority over your life at home. To rebel in our communication against our parents is to dishonor God. Just because they may not be easy to talk to does not give us the go-ahead to lessen our character as young believers. Take the time to genuinely listen to what they have to say, even in a casual conversation. We never get too old to care what Mom or Dad is feeling or thinking, whether we agree with it or not. It has been a long journey in this area with my Mom. For a long time, we thought we were communicating by arguing, and it resulted in a lot of hurt and bitterness. Then one day, I went to God and said, "God, I know I am in no way honoring you by the way I speak to my mother. Even though she has said things to hurt me, nonetheless, I know this is not the kind of relationship you ask us to have. God, will you teach me to communicate with my mother and will you teach her the same?" After I shared my prayer with my mom, she broke down and agreed. We started to apply love, respect, and genuine listening to our conversations. Let me say that God has blessed our relationship tremendously.

Of course, we still have some intense disagreements and much to learn, but it has been nowhere near the same as the past.

Maybe some of you are in a point in your life where you need to be obedient to God's voice. Life is so busy, you have full-time school, activities, even being involved in ministry, and throughout this, you know God has been tugging at your heart to just stop and have some alone time with Him. When was the last time you spent a sincere five minutes with God? How about a day? God is the one who wakes us up every morning and breathes breath into our nostrils to keep us going. He longs to be with us. He can't wait to have your full attention, because He has so much forgiveness to give you, so much grace to share with you, and so much to teach you about what you need to live in this dark world. Even if you start with just five minutes, a sincere five minutes, it will turn into a desire to have more and more time with the lover of your soul.

CHAPTER 10

Ambassadors of Christ

What if you represented Christ everywhere you went and with everyone you met? Take on the role of representation! If you think about the word *representation* and how it fits in with humanity, you will come to conclude that everyone represents something. Some of you represent work or it may be school or your family name. Many represent several things in this life. I used to work at a middle school, and one day, I saw the principal get on the intercom and say, "Students, I need you to be on your best behavior because we are going to have guests today and you don't want to misrepresent your school." Brothers and sisters, Paul told us something very similar in 2 Corinthians 5:20: "We are, therefore, Christ's ambassadors, as though God were making His appeal through us." Paul is talking about the ministry of reconciliation. He says if you have believed that Jesus Christ died for your sins and was raised to life, and through faith in Him alone you too have eternal life; the old has gone and the new has come. You are therefore Christ's ambassadors! You now represent something far greater and worthy than anything in this universe. You are now making an appeal on behalf of the name that is above every name, and we are to do that everywhere we go and to everyone we meet. It's not an easy thing. There are things in this life that hinder us from being that representation. We are going to look at two of the most common ones: fear and a lack of training. Then we are going to see how God addresses these.

We are going to start with Exodus 3 and 4. It's amazing how God has been sending out His people to represent Him even all the way back to the time of Moses. We think about Moses and we think of this great Biblical hero, which he was, but we are going to see how even this hero struggled with the same things you and I struggle with today when representing God. At this time, the Israelites are enslaved in Egypt, and they start crying out to God. He indeed hears their cry and is ready to deliver them from the hand of the Egyptians. This is where God appears to Moses in the burning bush, and we pick up their conversation in verse 10. God tells Moses, "So now go. I am sending you to Pharaoh to bring my people, the Israelites, out of Egypt." We see that God sends His people out with a purpose. He sends Moses to bring His people out of Egypt. God had a purpose for sending out Moses, and God has a purpose for sending you out. God continues to lay out the plan for Moses. He tells him, "This is what you are going to do, this is what you are going to say, and this is how you are going to do and say it."

Then we see Moses's immediate response in chapter 4 verse 1. (I encourage you to read chapter 4:1-15 so you may see the full picture of what is happening.) Moses answered, "What if they do not believe me or listen, and they say, 'The Lord did not appear to you'?" Moses's immediate response is fear of rejection, which is something we still struggle with today. We want to go talk to someone about our faith, but we are afraid of what they may say. Or we want to invite friends to church or Bible study, but we don't because we are afraid they will reject us.

God addresses this fear in verse 9. After telling Moses what three miraculous signs to perform, God then tells him something very interesting. He says, "But if they do not believe these two signs or listen to you, take some water from the Nile and pour it on dry ground." God gives Moses the heads up. He says, "Look, buddy, I am telling you right now, after you perform the first miraculous sign, you probably will get rejected; therefore, you will have to perform the second, and after that you may have to perform the third. Moses, you may get rejected not once but twice." God has given us the heads up. As Christ's ambassadors, we can expect rejection at times.

Jesus gave his disciples the heads up. He told them, "If the world hates you, keep in mind that it hated me first. (John 15:18)." He goes on to tell them that he has warned them so they can remember when the time comes (John 16:4). I am sure you have been rejected in things of this life. I know I have! You're still going, still here! Truth is, when it comes to Christ and the Word of God, people are not rejecting you. They are rejecting God! Even after God gives Moses the warning, we still see Moses's fear played out. In verse 10, Moses says, "O Lord, I have never been eloquent, neither in the past nor since you have spoken to your servant. I am slow of speech and tongue." God replies, "Who gave man his mouth? Who makes him deaf or mute? Is it not I, the Lord? Now go, I will help you speak and will teach you what to say." So Moses took the first route in telling God his fears, and that didn't work, so he moved on, telling God his defects and why he is not the man for the job. We often tell God everything that is wrong with us and how we are not the person for the job. God is telling us, "As if I didn't already know. I knit you together in your mother's womb. I know your potential better than you know yourself." He knows what we are capable better than we know it. But our fear is still geared toward man and not God.

As loving as God is, he is a just God as well. There are consequences for disobeying Him when He has asked us to do something. Christ said, "Do not be afraid of those who kill the body but cannot kill the soul. Rather, be afraid of the One who can destroy both soul and body in Hell" (Matthew 10:28). We need to have a holy fear toward God and not fear what men may say or do. After witnessing that the first two routes did not work, Moses flat out tells God in verse 13, "I don't think your hearing me clearly, God. Please just send someone else to do it." God is telling him (again using my scriptural imagination), "I hear you clearly, Moses, but I don't think you're hearing me. I have chosen you, and you are the man for the job." Then God tells Moses something very comforting in verse 15. He tells him that he will be with Moses and his brother the whole way. He is not just sending Moses out with a plan only to wait for him to get back.

Christ tells us the same comforting thing in Matthew 28:19-20. "All authoring in heaven and on earth has been given to me. Therefore go and make disciples of all nations, baptizing them in the name of the Father and of the Son and of the Holy Spirit . . . and lo I am with you always, to the very end of the age." I take that as, "John, every time you do something in my name, every time you step out, I am with you. Through the good times and especially the bad times, through thick and thin, lo I am with you." And not just to the end of the week or year, but to the very end. Lo, Christ is with us!

Now there are people who are not afraid of rejection, and they have a holy fear toward God, but they are hindered because a lack of training. When I think of the word *training*, I think of my high school football years. I remember reporting to practice, and each player would go to his position coach. Once we were there, we would practice the necessary drills for that position. There were times when someone did not show up to a practice or two. If one player reports to practice every day and practices the drills hard, and another player misses two days but practices the same drills, who is the coach more likely to use? Better yet, who is more likely to carry out his purpose on the field? As Christians, our preparation helps us accomplish our purpose.

Here are some practical spiritual drills that we can do. Maybe for some of you, it's starting off the day in prayer. Often, we wake up and we are so wrapped up in getting ready, thinking of what we have to do, and it doesn't cross our mind to thank God for another day of life. Be intentional in giving God your first thoughts of the day. Pray for others, pray for yourself, pray for opportunities for God to use you. After all, it is God who allows you to open your eyes every day and continues to breathe life into you. Maybe the drill is working toward reconciliation of a broken friendship or brother/sister hood. Have you asked for forgiveness? Or maybe you need to be the one to offer forgiveness. Start now and forgive, just as Christ forgave you. Another would be finally taking that bold step toward sharing your faith with that one person who you have been hesitant with for a long time. You caught yourself in a conversation with him and told yourself, "I am going to share now," but you didn't. Share your faith with him now and drop the seed. The drill may be joining a community of believers who are sharpening each other through the study of God's Word and fellowship. You may have been telling yourself that you will do just fine reading God's Word alone, and you don't need to be in fellowship with other believers. Of course, God will still teach you when you have your alone time with Him, but true spiritual Christian growth happens through being in community with other believers.

Now, that's not to say that God needs growth, but He displays perfect holy community within Himself: God the Father, God the Son, and God the Holy Spirit. All three are perfect in glory and perfect in community! One of the best things that we can do as Christ's ambassadors is to be intentional and real with people. Representing Christ is not just sharing the gospel, but living it as well. What opportunities do you have around you to be a light in this dark world? It's not doing something fancy, either, but just being intentional and real with others. For example, our church partners with the local fire department to help them with their annual barbeque fundraiser (we currently meet at their fire hall). I shared with the congregation how this was a perfect opportunity to live the gospel by volunteering to help them. If we see these opportunities as just events, then we are right: they are just events. But God's Word says in all things you do, do as if you are working for God and for His glory (Colossian 3:17). They needed help in cutting the meat, serving all the sides, and so forth. You may ask, "Well how does serving potato salad onto a plate and passing it on bring glory to God?" It's not so much the action of serving potato salad, rather it's the condition of your heart in the midst of it all. Once your heart tells God, "I am doing this for your glory by serving these people, and I gladly do it," those scoops of potato salad are no longer just scoops of potato salad; they're scoops of glory. So if you eat, you bring glory to God. If you talk, you bring glory to God, and if you have an opportunity to serve in any way, you bring glory to God.

One day, as I was going through this passage of being an ambassador of Christ, I asked God to show me what it truly means to do so. I asked for opportunities to come my way. Well, a couple of days later, I went through a drive-through at a restaurant where I know the owner, management, and most of the employees. Now, most of the time when I order inside, I joke with the cashiers. One of the common jokes I pull is if they get my order wrong or made a mistake, I say, "Ahh I'm going to tell the owner." They joke back and say, "Oh go ahead, whatever." It always seems to brighten moments up. Well, as I went through the drive-through, I ordered this sauce that I like. When I pulled up to the window and got my food, the first thing I looked for was the sauce. When I saw it was not in the bag, I asked the employee for some and she said they had run out as it was near closing time. I didn't know this employee, and so I asked her if she can check in the back, because I knew they would sometimes carry a reserve. Sure enough, she came back with the sauce, and I said, "Ahh, you lied. I'm going to tell the owner," and then started laughing. When I looked at her, she wasn't laughing. She said, "Thank you," and closed the window. As I drove off, I told my younger sister, who was with me, that I was concerned that I might have upset the employee.

The next morning, I called the manager and told him what had happened, and he said, "Oh yeah, John, I was going to call you and ask you what happened because as soon as you drove off, she went to the back and started to cry, thinking she was going to lose her job." Right then, my heart fell, and of course, I felt horrible. I told him how I pulled the joke with her but she must have taken it seriously. I asked him if she was going to work that day so I could pass by and apologize and ask her to forgive me. He said yes, and for me to come by later in the day when I got out of work. Five o'clock came around, I got out of work, and started heading toward the restaurant, when a fear built up inside of me. I started telling God how I was nervous that this girl might not want to talk to me. I said, "What if she just turns her back when she sees me? Man, what if she slaps me?" Then I started to think of an excuse to tell the manager why I wouldn't be able to make it. Right there, I remembered the Corinthians passage, and the words hit me: "Are you going to let this opportunity pass by because of some little fear of rejection you have? You have this opportunity to be a light and witness to this young girl." I told God, "I'm sorry, God. Yes, I will go." I walked into the store, and when they told her that I was there, I could see she hesitated a little, but she still walked over. I told her, "I am so sorry for last night. It was not my intention to hurt you in any way. Please forgive me."

With tears in her eyes, she said, "Wow, I have never seen a guy do that. Yes, of course I forgive you." People are hurting every day. People are on the edge of depression and suicide every day. People need to be loved every day. My question to you is: what are you going to do? Because I can guarantee you, the moment you stop reading this book, many opportunities are going to come your way. Are you going to let fear of man or missing out on your spiritual drills hinder you from representing well? Or are you going to seize the opportunity? Think of the impact it would have on this world if you represented Christ everywhere you go and to everyone you meet.

CHAPTER 11

For the Glory of God

I think it is vital not only for the believer in Christ, but simply for the human soul, to live in humility. Christ painted the perfect picture by showing the full extent of His humility and how we need to walk that same way. Mankind has lived in the complete opposite way for far too long; that is pride. Pride has caused the rise and fall of many presidents and rulers. It has caused the fall of many countries through bloodshed. It has caused violent acts among us for way too long. Pride has simply caused people to not follow Christ. The Apostle Paul said that no one else in history has expressed the importance of humility better than Christ. Philippians 2:5 says, "Your attitude should be the same as that of Christ Jesus." Any attitude that does not reflect Christ is not of God and should not be used by the believer. This old idea that "I woke up on the wrong side of the bed, therefore I'm entitled to have a bad attitude" seriously needs to be thrown out the window for good. I hear this, and I tell the person he missed the point. It's not whether you woke up on the wrong or right side. Rather, what is important is that you woke up, and God has a reason for making that happen. What about that attitude that goes something like this: "It has been a long day. I don't care. I don't want to hear it; just leave me alone." Can you imagine if God took on the same attitude when we pray to Him? "Father, I need your help right now. I need a lending ear." I couldn't imagine how one might react if God responded, "Not now. I've had a long thousands of years. I've been helping the wounded in Iraq, empowering the speaker in China, comforting the widow in New York, and listening to prayers all over this earth." If anyone knows what it is to have a long day, it's God. If Christ, in all His busyness, did not display this type of attitude toward others, what gives us the right?

Growing up, I had a horrible attitude. I yelled a lot, argued, and even fought. When I received Christ as my Lord and Savior, boy was I excited. I told myself, "I need to learn how to pray and start reading the Bible." God had a slightly different plan for the start of my journey. It seemed like God had said something like this: "The first thing I'm going to do is get rid of this stinking attitude of yours." This did not happen overnight, but there was much improvement as I did my best to submit to God and pursue humility, which I still have to do on a daily basis.

Continuing in Philippians 2:6-8 it says, "Who, being in very nature God, did not consider equality with God something to be grasped, but made himself nothing, taking the very nature of a servant, being made in human likeness. And being found in appearance as a man, he humbled himself and became obedient to death, even death on a cross." Paul is painting an amazing picture here. Christ was in perfect glory with God before He came in the flesh. But He did not hold on selfishly to everything He had. I could almost imagine the words the Father had. "Son, it's going to take a perfect sacrifice, and there is no one on earth that is perfect." Christ Jesus took off His royal robe and crowns, walked across the kingdom of heaven, and humbly left His position of high authority and power. What strikes me even more amazing is how Christ continued to humble Himself. Although He could have been born in a castle like a king, He was born in a manger. The Scripture records that He didn't even have a place to lay His head. If you take a look around, you can see why Paul stressed the need for us to live in humility. He knew that far too many people would journey through this life on a high horse. We would be conceited and often not care about the needs of others. This is not the way of Christ! Christ's humility played out till His last breath. He could have stopped Judas from betraying Him, but He didn't. He could have called legions of angels to save Him when He was being arrested, but He didn't. He could have retaliated when the soldiers mocked him, but He didn't. While nailed to the cross, He could have come down and walked away, but in perfect obedience to God, He didn't. This was done for the glory of God!

Count the Cost

Have you ever seen the movie *John Q* (one of my favorites, by the way)? It's the story of a young boy who collapses at his baseball game and, when taken to the hospital, his parents find out that he has a heart condition that will require a transplant. His father, played by Denzel Washington, works at a factory, and his mother works at a grocery store; they're your average hardworking family. During the meeting with the surgeon and the person running the hospital, John Q and his wife are informed of the condition of their son. They are told that if he does not get a new heart, their son will die. So they begin to weigh the option of whether or not to do the surgery. They decide to go ahead with it and are told that their son's name should go right to the top of the donor list. Just then, the lady running the hospital interrupts and says, "Wait, it's not that easy. There are certain fees that have to be met before his name gets on that list." John Q replies, "We've got insurance." It turns out that John Q's insurance policy does not cover a surgery of this magnitude. His next question is vital here: "Well, how much does it cost?" "Two hundred and fifty thousand," she says. Of course, he is taken aback. This is a question that we need to ask ourselves when it comes to following Jesus: what does it cost? Not for the purpose of whether or not we should pursue the cost, but rather for the purpose of doing our very best to fulfill the cost. We live in a world where we have to pay, whether with money or time. Just like John Q, some of you may be taken aback by the cost that Jesus set for us to be his disciples. Thank God it's not two hundred and fifty thousand dollars! He set a cost that each and every one of us can meet: the cost is ourselves!

Luke 14:25-27 reads, "Large crowds were traveling with Jesus and turning to them he said: 'If anyone comes to me and does not hate his father and mother, his wife and children, his brother and sisters—yes, even his own life—he cannot be my disciple. And anyone who does not carry his cross and follow me cannot be my disciple.'" So large crowds are following Jesus, and He turns to them and says, "Look, there are many of you following me, and I'm telling you right now, it's not going to be this easy." If you think about it, we can see why many would want to follow Jesus everywhere He went. He was the guy to be around. You would have front-row tickets to all the miracles and healings, and all the fish and bread you could eat when He multiplied it. It is as if Jesus turned around and said, "Many of you seriously need to check yourself." I wonder, would Christ have the same words for me? Would He have the same words for you? I can't look to my left or right; I can only analyze my heart. Now, He also said, if anyone does not hate his family, even his own life, they could not be His disciple. Did He mean *hate* literally? Many other places in Scripture, He talks about loving God and loving others. What He is saying is love is a priority. To *hate* here means simply to love less. You must love Him above your parents, your wife and children; you must love Christ more than life itself! Here He is speaking to men, for he says "more than your wife," but the principle is the same for all believers. If you want to be a true disciple of Christ, your love and loyalty to Him must be far above anything and everyone else.

Let me ask you, if tonight while you are asleep, you hear a voice calling your name, and you know it's Jesus, and He says, "I want you to get up, move your family (or yourself) to Haiti, and start an orphanage," would you go? Jesus is saying that in order for us to be His disciple, the answer always needs to be yes. The truth is, this probably will not happen to many of you, but it certainly is possible if Christ so chooses to ask you. I'm going to turn it up a few notches. What if Christ told you the same thing tonight, but added, "And you might not make it back. I am sending you to a country where persecution is high." Would you go? Maybe Christ will not call you to such loyalty, but He has in the past. Especially right now, high rates of persecution toward Christians are going on in different parts of the world. We can only ask ourselves, "Am I willing to pay the price?"

Christ continued in verse 27, "And anyone who does not carry his cross and follow me cannot be my disciple." Again, did He mean that literally? Imagine what that would look like. Picture two guys walking along, and one tells the other, "So, you are a follower of Christ, huh?" And the other replies yes. "So I am assuming you're pretty loyal to him?"

JOHN E. BARBA

The guy replies, "Sometimes, but I do carry this four-foot cross (and actually pulls one out of the trunk of his car) with me everywhere I go, because that's what true disciples do." No! In Jesus' days, when the Romans would sentence a criminal to crucifixion, often he was forced to carry his cross through the heart of the city and to the execution site. This was a public display that the Romans were right in their sentencing. Luke recorded Christ's words here, but added the word *daily*. When we are obeying His commands, which are loving God and loving others, forgiving, being in humble spirits, and not denying His way, we are carrying our cross. Jesus knew that we would not want to do these things on a daily basis. We would fall short! Think about it. There are many times when we don't want to forgive or love sacrificially, much less do it on a daily basis. When we do, just like the man who publicly carries his cross, saying the Romans are right, our life publicly speaks out and says, "Jesus is right, and I follow him."

Consider the idea of buying a car. Have you ever gone to a dealership and tried to negotiate the price until it seriously came down? Sometimes, they won't bring that price down, and you need to consider the full price. If we want to be true disciples of Christ, we must consider the full price. There's no bargaining here! Often, we try to bargain our loyalty to Christ. "Okay, Jesus, I'll give you Monday, Wednesday, and Friday but not Tuesday, Thursday, or the weekend," is a common thought among Christians. But Christ said, "Carry it daily." I know I have tried to bargain; however, we can seriously get stubborn. He is not going to bring down the price and has clearly said daily. Here is why: Christ will settle for nothing less than all of you. He loves all of you and desires all of you. The cross paid all of it for all of you! Are we willing to sacrifice everything if the situation calls for it? I hope so! If all His children armed themselves with that kind of attitude, I couldn't begin to think of how the Kingdom of God would be impacted for eternity. What if we just came to the point in our lives where we told Jesus, "Forgive me for all this bargaining that I have done. I don't want it anymore. I want you on a daily basis." Ask Him to help you with any unbelief, and He will meet you and change you. He will put you into a heart-pounding, mind-blowing, soul-driving relationship with Him. Count the cost!